KV-578-193

Saint Martin

Novena and Prayers

By the Daughters of St. Paul

Pauline
BOOKS & MEDIA
Boston

Nihil Obstat: Rev. John J. Connelly, S.T.D.
Imprimatur: ✠ Bernard Cardinal Law
Archbishop of Boston
July 5, 2001

ISBN 0-8198-7060-9

Cover art: Anna Leliwa

Texts of the New Testament used in this work are taken from The *St. Paul Catholic Edition of the New Testament,* translated by Mark A. Wauck. Copyright © 1992, Society of St. Paul. All rights reserved.

Texts of the Psalms used in this work are translated by Manuel Miguens. Copyright © 1995, Daughters of St. Paul.

Copyright © 2002, Daughters of St. Paul

Published by Pauline Books & Media, 50 Saint Pauls Avenue, Boston MA 02130-3491.

Printed in the U.S.A.

www.pauline.org

Pauline Books & Media is the publishing house of the Daughters of St. Paul, an international congregation of women religious serving the Church with the communications media.

2 3 4 5 6 7   13 12 11 10 09

Contents

What Is a Novena?

The Catholic tradition of praying novenas has its roots in the earliest days of the Church. In the Acts of the Apostles we read that after the ascension of Jesus, the apostles returned to Jerusalem, to the upper room, where "They all devoted themselves single-mindedly to prayer, along with some women and Mary the Mother of Jesus and his brothers" (Acts 1:14). Jesus had instructed his disciples to wait for the coming of the Holy Spirit, and on the day of Pentecost, the Spirit of the Lord came to them. This prayer of the first Christian community was the first "novena." Based on this, Christians have always prayed for various needs, trusting that God both hears and answers prayer.

The word "novena" is derived from the Latin term *novem*, meaning nine. In biblical times numbers held deep symbolism for people. The number "three," for example, symbolized perfection, fullness, completeness. The number nine—three times

5

three—symbolized perfection times perfection. Novenas developed because it was thought that—symbolically speaking—nine days represented the perfect amount of time to pray. The ancient Greeks and Romans had the custom of mourning for nine days after a death. The early Christian Church offered Mass for the deceased for nine consecutive days. During the Middle Ages novenas in preparation for solemn feasts became popular, as did novenas to particular saints.

Whether a novena is made solemnly—in a parish church in preparation for a feastday—or in the privacy of one's home, as Christians we never really pray alone. Through the waters of Baptism we have become members of the body of Christ and are thereby united to every other member of Christ's Mystical Body. When we pray, we are spiritually united with all the other members.

Just as we pray for each other while here on earth, those who have gone before us and are united with God in heaven can pray for us and intercede for us as well. We Catholics use the term "communion of saints" to refer to this exchange of spiritual help among the members of the Church on earth, those who have died and are being purified, and the saints in heaven.

While nothing can replace the celebration of Mass and the sacraments as the Church's highest form of prayer, devotions have a special place in Catholic life. Devotions such as the stations of the cross can help us enter into the sufferings of Jesus and give us an understanding of his personal love for us. The mysteries of the rosary can draw us into meditating on the lives of Jesus and Mary. Devotions to the saints can help us witness to our faith and encourage us in our commitment to lead lives of holiness and service as they did.

———— ❧ ————

How to use this booklet

The morning and evening prayers are modeled on the Liturgy of the Hours, following its pattern of psalms, scripture readings and intercessions.

We suggest that during the novena you make time in your schedule to pray the morning prayer and evening prayer. If you are able, try to also set aside a time during the day when you can pray the novena and any other particular prayer(s) you have chosen. Or you can recite the devotional prayers at the conclusion of the morning or evening prayer. What is important is to pray with expectant faith and confidence in a loving God who will answer our prayers in the way that will most benefit us. The Lord "satisfies the thirsty, and the hungry he fills with good things" (Ps 107:9).

St. Martin de Porres

*B*orn in Lima, Peru in 1579, Martin de Porres was the son of a Spanish knight and a Panamanian woman of color named Ana Velazquez. The father, Juan, abandoned the family for a while when Martin was a child, although he later cared for the boy and provided him with a tutor. Martin then became an apprentice to a pharmacist, where he learned a good bit about medicine. Even as a boy Martin wanted to help the needy, and he gave away food to the homeless despite his own poverty. He saw Christ in the face of the hungry who asked for something to eat.

The Dominican Fathers staffed a church in Lima dedicated to Our Lady of the Rosary, where Martin often went to pray. Eventually he asked if he could live at the monastery as a lay helper and was admitted. In his humility he wanted to remain a tertiary, but after a few years he decided to become a religious brother, a choice his superiors encouraged him to make.

After professing his vows in 1603, Martin was assigned to the infirmary, where he put his medical knowledge and skills to good use. He cared not only for the Dominicans who were ill, but also for all those who asked for his help. Word soon spread around the city that Martin assisted anyone who needed assistance, and soon more and more people flocked to the monastery.

Before distributing food, Martin always gave it a special blessing: "May the Lord bless and increase this food, and may he sanctify all who eat it." No matter how little food was on hand, Martin never sent anyone away hungry. One day when Martin took the last piece of bread from the pantry, the cook complained to the superior, who answered, "Do not worry. Martin will not finish it. There will still be enough for all of us too." And so it happened. No matter how much Martin gave away, God always provided enough for everybody.

Besides his active social work, Martin developed a deep love of prayer. He often prayed through the night, especially when he was keeping watch on someone in the infirmary. Martin also had a deep devotion to the Blessed Mother and promoted the rosary.

His kindness extended to all of God's creatures. One day when he came across an injured dog, he brought it home, nursed it back to health and returned it to its owner. When mice began to damage the vestments in the sacristy, the superior told Martin to get rid of them. Not wanting to kill them, he called them together and led them to the barn, where he fed them.

Martin served God as a Dominican for forty-five years, lovingly caring for the sick, the poor and homeless children. After a lifetime of hard work and social service, he died in November 1639. He is invoked as the patron of African-Americans and of social justice.

Morning Prayer

*M*orning prayer is a time to give praise and thanks to God, to remind ourselves that he is the source of all beauty and goodness. Lifting one's heart and mind to God in the early hours of the day puts one's life into perspective: God is our loving Creator who watches over us with tenderness and is always ready to embrace us with his compassion and mercy.

While at prayer, try to create a prayerful atmosphere, perhaps with a burning candle to remind you that Christ is the light who illumines your daily path, an open Bible to remind you that the Lord is always present, a crucifix to remind you of the depths of God's love for you. Soft music can also contribute to a serene and prayerful mood.

If a quiet place is not available, or if you pray as you commute to and from work, remember that the God who loves you is present everywhere and hears your prayer no matter the setting.

I will bless the Lord at all times.
His praise will be ever on my lips.
Glory to the Father, and to the Son, and to the
Holy Spirit,
As it was in the beginning, is now, and will be
forever. Amen.

Psalm 103

Let all creation praise God's holy name.

Bless the LORD, my soul;
all my being, bless his holy name.
Bless the LORD, my soul,
and let not all his kindnesses be forgotten:
he forgives all your guilt;
he heals all your infirmities;
he rescues your life from the grave;
he crowns you with loving kindness and tender love;
he bestows fulfilling goodness upon your years.
Your youthfulness is thus renewed, like an eagle's.
He does righteous deeds
and rules in favor of all the oppressed.
He discloses his ways to Moses,
his accomplishments to the children of Israel.
The LORD is compassionate and gracious,
slow to anger and rich in loving kindness.
Glory to the Father....

Psalm 25

The Lord is my light and my salvation.

To you, O LORD, I lift up my soul
In you my God I trust: I shall not be disappointed,
my enemies shall not rejoice at my expense.
Indeed, none of those shall be disappointed who
   rely on you.
Give me knowledge of your ways, O LORD;
instruct me in your paths.
Make me walk in your truth and teach me.
Because you are my saving God,
it is on you that I have relied at all times.
Glory to the Father....

The Word of God   Matthew 25:34–36

*People come into our life, sometimes daily, asking
for our time and resources. Let us welcome them as we
would welcome the Lord, and, in the process, we will
find God's reward.*

*C*ome you blessed of my Father, receive the
Kingdom prepared for you from the foun-
dation of the world, for I was hungry and you gave
me to eat; I was thirsty and you gave me to drink; I

was a stranger and you took me in, naked and you clothed me, sick and you took care of me, I was in prison and you came to me.

Give me knowledge of your ways, O Lord.

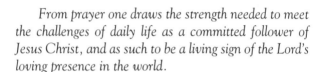

From prayer one draws the strength needed to meet the challenges of daily life as a committed follower of Jesus Christ, and as such to be a living sign of the Lord's loving presence in the world.

Intercessions

*F*ather in heaven, we celebrate your gift of a new day. With joy in your loving presence, I entrust to you my needs today and pray:

Response: *Lord, be my light and my salvation.*

Inspire my thoughts, words and actions so that all I do and say may be pleasing to you and serve your kingdom here on earth. **R.**

Prepare my heart to meet you in my neighbors and coworkers. **R.**

Be with me so that I may recognize the opportunities you give me to reach out to others in your name. **R.**

Help me to use the gifts and talents you have given me to generously and lovingly serve others who are in need. **R.**

Grant that I may spend this day in joy of spirit and peace of mind. **R.**

(Add your own general intentions and your particular intention for this novena.)

Conclude your intercessions by praying to our Heavenly Father in the words Jesus taught us:

Our Father, who art in heaven, hallowed be thy name; thy kingdom come; thy will be done on earth as it is in heaven. Give us this day our daily bread, and forgive us our trespasses, as we forgive those who trespass against us, and lead us not into temptation, but deliver us from evil. Amen.

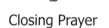

Closing Prayer

*L*ord, let the splendor of your love light my way. As I begin this day in dedication to you, keep me true to your teaching and free from all sin. I ask this through Jesus Christ, your Son. Amen.

Let us praise the Lord

And give him thanks.

Novena to
St. Martin de Porres

First Day

Ask! and it shall be given to you; Seek! and you will find; Knock! and it shall be opened to you (Mt 7:7).

Martin took to heart the promise of Jesus and approached his loving Father with a humble heart, praising and thanking the Lord, asking with great confidence for the graces he needed.

St. Martin, sometimes the concerns of every day living consume all my energies and I forget that the Lord is present with me, to help and guide me. I want to lift my heart in praise to God and thank him for all the blessings he has given me, but most of the time this desire remains only a passing thought. I need your help, your inspiration.

Teach me how to be a prayerful person, how to set aside time for prayer, how to turn my daily activities into a prayer of praise and gratitude.

Lord Jesus, grant me the gift of a humble and confident heart, a heart ready to embrace your word in Scripture, a heart ready to love and serve others in your name.

———

Our Father, who art in heaven, hallowed be thy name; thy kingdom come; thy will be done on earth as it is in heaven. Give us this day our daily bread, and forgive us our trespasses, as we forgive those who trespass against us, and lead us not into temptation, but deliver us from evil. Amen.

———

Hail Mary, full of grace, the Lord is with you. Blessed are you among women, and blessed is the fruit of your womb, Jesus. Holy Mary, Mother of God, pray for us sinners, now and at the hour of our death. Amen.

Glory to the Father, and to the Son, and to the Holy Spirit, As it was in the beginning, is now, and will be forever. Amen.

St. Martin, pray for us.

Second Day

Blessed are the poor in spirit, for theirs is the kingdom of heaven (Mt 5:3).

Martin was called "the father of the poor" because he not only gave alms to the poor, but he treated them with compassion and respect. His knowledge of healing remedies served him in practical ways to treat the sick and to comfort and console the dying.

St. Martin, teach me how to give importance to the things that really matter in life—family, church, friends, neighbors—and to be the love of Christ for others. Show me how to live in gratitude to God for all he has given me, to acknowledge that our generous and loving Lord has given me everything I have.

Jesus, Lord, grant me a generous heart to see the needs of those who have less than I, and a willing spirit to give without counting the cost.

Our Father, Hail Mary, Glory

St. Martin, pray for us.

Third Day

Blessed are those who are mourning, for they shall be comforted (Mt 5:4).

Martin placed his trust in the goodness and promises of God. He offered God his ordinary daily works as prayers of intercession for others, namely the poor, the sick and the oppressed. Martin saw in them the face of the suffering Jesus, and tried, through his own simple words and deeds, to console and encourage those around him, especially those who had no one to care for them.

St. Martin, teach me how to remove the barriers of self-centeredness that prevent me from loving and serving others, especially those with whom I live and work, those in my neighborhood and church community. Help me to understand and take to heart the Gospel message that whatever I do to others, I do to Jesus.

Lord Jesus, grant me a willing spirit so that in word and deed I may promote the dignity of every human person. May my words and actions encourage and comfort those around me who may be hurting or in pain. Lord, let me be your loving presence for others until the day that I rejoice with you and all the saints in heaven.

Our Father, Hail Mary, Glory

St. Martin, pray for us.

———————— ❧ ————————

Fourth Day

Blessed are the meek for they shall inherit the earth (Mt 5:5).

Martin accepted his creaturehood and honored God as Creator and Father of all. He understood the love that God has for his creatures, and that God has the well-being of his children at heart. Martin had the spiritual wisdom to recognize this truth, to give his life over to God's providential care, offering praise and worship to the Lord of Love. He attributed all the good works that he accomplished in his lifetime to the grace of God working in and through him.

St. Martin, teach me how to recognize my limitations, to acknowledge my dependence on God and accept his unconditional love for me. Help me to put aside whatever may injure my relationship with Jesus or my loved ones. Inspire me so that I may better see and cherish the gifts God has given to me in my family and friends.

Lord Jesus, you know the depths of my heart— my desires, fears and heartaches. Grant me a meek and humble heart that I may know how to rely on your love and seek happiness in doing your will. Amen.

Our Father, Hail Mary, Glory

St. Martin, pray for us.

Fifth Day

Blessed are those who hunger and thirst to do God's will, for they shall have their fill (Mt 5:6).

Martin spent his time on earth doing good for others in whatever way he could as a Dominican brother. He coped with the difficulties, discomforts and sufferings that life brought to him, but he had learned how to keep his gaze fixed on the faithful love of Jesus, and desired to be with him in heaven. This is the heroism that we acknowledge and celebrate in Martin's life.

St. Martin, teach me how to keep my focus on Jesus when problems seem to engulf me. Show me how to sort through my worries and concerns. Ask the Lord to grant me the wisdom to know what is right and to follow it, so that I may be a true disciple of Jesus.

Lord Jesus, be my rock and fortress amid the difficulties of life. Teach me the power and truth of your word and let it guide me so that I may always do your will. Amen.

Our Father, Hail Mary, Glory

St. Martin, pray for us.

Sixth Day

Blessed are the merciful for they shall receive mercy (Mt 5:7).

Martin often worked under difficult conditions to assist the needy, but others did not always appreciate and accept his efforts to help them. At times this caused him suffering, but it did not prevent him from carrying out his works of charity and healing. Taking Jesus as his model, he learned how to forgive those who wronged him and even prayed for them.

St. Martin, help me to love and care for those around me even when they may not appreciate or accept my efforts. Inspire me to imitate Jesus' love especially when dealing with difficult people.

Heavenly Father, remove from my heart all resentment and anger. Grant me the grace to repent of my sins and to forgive others just as you have generously forgiven me. Amen.

Our Father, Hail Mary, Glory

St. Martin, pray for us.

Seventh Day

Blessed are the pure of heart, they shall see God (Mt 5:8).

The fire of God's love inflamed Martin, filling him with spiritual gifts. He realized that God had granted humanity his greatest gift by sending his Son into the world to redeem us. This thought awakened in Martin such a profound love for God that his whole life reflected his gratitude. Whatever he did, he did for the Lord.

St. Martin, teach me how to focus my life on the things of God. Show me how to walk the path of gratitude so that I may acknowledge and appreciate life's simple gifts, which the Lord has given to me and my loved ones.

Lord Jesus, let your love burn within my heart so that I may love all those I call family and neighbor with the same love you have shown me. May

my love for them bring healing, comfort and peace.
Amen.

Our Father, Hail Mary, Glory

St. Martin, pray for us.

Eighth Day

Blessed are the peacemakers, for they shall be called children of God (Mt 5:9).

Martin performed many miracles even during his life here on earth. He used this great gift of God to bring healing and hope to the poor, the sick and the suffering. His intimate relationship with the Lord gave him such great inner peace that he became God's instrument to show others how to find peace of heart.

St. Martin, teach me how to find peace of heart so that I may be God's instrument of peace among my family, friends, neighbors and coworkers. Help me to listen to others with an open mind, to nurture tolerance in myself and others and grow in a non-judgmental attitude.

Lord Jesus, grant me the grace to live true to your commands so that your peace may reign in my heart. May your kingdom come in my life and in the lives of all those I meet today. Amen.

Our Father, Hail Mary, Glory

St. Martin, pray for us.

———— ✖ ————

Ninth Day

Blessed are those persecuted for doing God's will, for theirs is the kingdom of heaven (Mt 5:10).

At times Martin was ill-treated because of his commitment to the needs of the poor and the suffering. Rather than allowing criticism to discourage him and prevent him from doing good, he accepted it as a challenge. When he met persons who did not understand his dedication to the sick and needy, Martin tried to respond as Jesus would. He strove for a closer following of Christ, who was also misunderstood and rejected for doing good works.

St. Martin, teach me how to continue to walk the path of integrity, kindness and patience when others misjudge my good intentions and actions. Show me how to respond to those who might ridicule me for not joining in gossip or off-color conversations.

Lord Jesus, grant me the grace to look beyond my present sufferings and to rejoice in the new life that awaits me with you and the saints in heaven.

Let me learn to forgive and to see your hand at work in all things.

Our Father, Hail Mary, Glory

St. Martin, pray for us.

Prayers for Various Needs

Prayer to Martin de Porres
for the Virtue of Charity

*M*ost glorious St. Martin de Porres, we invoke your intercession and honor you for your ardent charity, which embraced not only your needy brothers and sisters, but all God's creatures, even the animals of the field.

From your throne in heaven we ask you to listen to the petitions of your brothers and sisters in need. By imitating your virtues may we live in joy, happy to follow in the footsteps of our Redeemer and his Mother, carrying our daily cross with strength and courage until the day we reach the kingdom of heaven through the merits of our Savior, Jesus Christ. Amen.

Prayer to St. Martin de Porres
for Interracial Harmony

*S*t. Martin, your love for all of God's people gives us confidence to ask you to intercede for us, so that men and women of every race may value the gifts of culture and tradition that each possesses. May we act only and always with respect, kindness and tolerance toward one another, doing our utmost to preserve the unity among peoples which the Spirit gives through the gift of peace and reconciliation. Amen.

Prayer to St. Martin de Porres
in Time of Need

*G*lorious St. Martin de Porres, we thank and praise God for your inspiring example of charity. Your self-sacrificing love embraced sick, suffering, poor and needy persons. Your concern for all God's creatures moved you to care for even the smallest and weakest animals of the field.

From your place in heaven among the saints, intercede to God for us who invoke you in our time of need (*mention your petition*). By imitating your examples of charity, goodness and patience may we have the grace to accept the difficulties and sufferings of life, relying also on the help of Mary, our Blessed Mother. May we know and feel that Jesus is with us in our pain, bringing us healing and hope. May the trials we face not blind us to the many blessings we also receive from the hands of our Heavenly Father as we look forward to the joys of heaven. Amen.

Prayer of Praise and Thanksgiving

It is fitting for us to praise and thank God for the graces and privileges he has bestowed upon the saints. Devotees of St. Martin de Porres may pray the following act of thanksgiving during their novena.

Lord Jesus, I praise, glorify and bless you for all the graces and privileges you have bestowed upon your servant and friend Martin de Porres. By his merits grant me your grace, and through his intercession help me in all my needs. At the hour of my death be with me until that time when I can join the saints in heaven to praise you forever and ever. Amen.

Evening Prayer

*A*s this day draws to a close we place ourselves in an attitude of thanksgiving. We take time to express our gratitude to a loving God for his abiding presence. We thank him for the gift of the day and all it brought with it. We thank him for all the things we were able to achieve throughout the day, and we entrust to him the concerns we have for tomorrow.

From the rising to the setting of the sun,
May the name of the Lord be praised.
Glory to the Father, and to the Son, and to the
    Holy Spirit,
As it was in the beginning, is now, and will be
    forever. Amen.

Take a few moments for a brief examination of conscience. Reflect on the ways God acted in your life today, how you responded to his invitations to think, speak and act in a more Christlike manner, and in what ways you would like to be a more faithful disciple tomorrow.

Lord, in your great love have mercy:

For the times I acted or spoke unkindly toward
others.

Lord, have mercy.

For the times I was not generous with my time and
talents.

Christ, have mercy.

For the times I was unwelcoming or unforgiving.

Lord, have mercy.

For the times…(any other petitions for pardon).

(Or any other Act of Sorrow.)

Psalm 8

Praise be to God forever

O LORD our God, how majestic is your name over
all the earth!

Your praise resounds above the heavens.

When I contemplate your heavens, the work of
your hands,

the moon and the stars, which you fixed in place,

What is mortal man that you should think of
him—

the son of man, that you should care for him?

Still, you have made him little less than the gods
and crowned him with glory and splendor.

You have given him dominion over the works of
        your hands;
all things you have set under his feet
all of the sheep and oxen,
but also untamed beasts,
birds of the air, and the fish of the sea.
O LORD our God, how majestic is your name
        over all the earth.
Glory to the Father....

The Word of God Matthew 15:30–31

*It is easy to see the Lord in the beauty of a sunrise
or sunset, or in extraordinary happenings. But we often
miss God in the ordinary events of life and common-
place people.*

Large crowds came to Jesus. They had with
them lame, blind, crippled, dumb people, and
many others, and they put them down at his feet
and he cured them, so that the crowd marveled
when they saw the dumb speaking, cripples sound,
the lame walking, and the blind seeing, and they
glorified God.

Glory to you, Lord, Source of all that is good.

In prayer we bring before the Lord our own needs and the needs of those we love. We take time to consider the needs of the world and intercede for those who do not or cannot pray. We offer petitions for the improvement of the human condition so that our world will be a better place to live, and all people may contribute to building up God's kingdom here on earth.

Intercessions

God of tender mercies, your goodness is without limit and we thank you for the blessings you have given us today. Confident in your wisdom and loving care, we present to you the needs of all your people.

Response: Lord, hear our prayer through the intercession of St. Martin de Porres.

For the shepherds of your Church and all those who minister in your name: may they be prudent in judgment and gentle in love, holy and true witnesses to your gospel. **R.**

For world leaders: may they govern with integrity and justice so that all peoples may live in peace and dignity. **R.**

For peoples of every nation, race, culture and religion: may harmony and kindness drive out prejudice and hatred. **R.**

For those who minister to the poor and needy: may they receive joy in this life and the fullness of joy in the life hereafter. **R.**

For the poor, the homeless, refugees and victims of natural disaster: may they find the help and support they need in their brothers and sisters, children of the same Heavenly Father. **R.**

For the elderly, the homebound and the terminally ill: may they find comfort in God's love for them, and support from compassionate friends and caregivers. **R.**

For all those who suffer in body, mind or spirit: may they experience the touch of the Divine Healer. R.

For the faithful departed: may they enjoy the peace and happiness of heaven. **R.**

(Add any other spontaneous intentions and your particular intentions for this novena.)

Conclude your intercessions by praying to our Heavenly Father in the words Jesus taught us:

Our Father, who art in heaven....

Closing Prayer

Gracious and loving God, receive my evening prayer and hear the needs of your people. May all who call upon you in faith experience your love and compassion. Grant this through Jesus Christ your Son. Amen.

Mary, Jesus' Mother and ours, is always ready to intercede for those who ask her help.

Hail Mary, full of grace, the Lord is with you. Blessed are you among women, and blessed is the fruit of your womb, Jesus. Holy Mary, Mother of God, pray for us sinners, now and at the hour of our death. Amen.

May God's blessing remain with us forever. In the name of the Father, and of the Son, and of the Holy Spirit. Amen.

Pauline
BOOKS & MEDIA

The Daughters of St. Paul operate book and media centers at the following addresses. Visit, call or write the one nearest you today, or find us on the World Wide Web, www.pauline.org

CALIFORNIA

    3908 Sepulveda Blvd, Culver City, CA 90230   310-397-8676

    2640 Broadway Street, Redwood City, CA 94063   650-369-4230

    5945 Balboa Avenue, San Diego, CA 92111   858-565-9181

FLORIDA

    145 S.W. 107th Avenue, Miami, FL 33174   305-559-6715

HAWAII

    1143 Bishop Street, Honolulu, HI 96813   808-521-2731

    Neighbor Islands call: 866-521-2731

ILLINOIS

    172 North Michigan Avenue, Chicago, IL 60601   312-346-4228

LOUISIANA

    4403 Veterans Memorial Blvd, Metairie, LA 70006   504-887-7631

MASSACHUSETTS

    885 Providence Hwy, Dedham, MA 02026   781-326-5385

MISSOURI

    9804 Watson Road, St. Louis, MO 63126   314-965-3512

NEW JERSEY

    561 U.S. Route 1, Wick Plaza, Edison, NJ 08817   732-572-1200

NEW YORK

    64 W. 38th Street, New York, NY 10018   212-754-1110

PENNSYLVANIA

    9171-A Roosevelt Blvd, Philadelphia, PA 19114   215-676-9494

SOUTH CAROLINA

    243 King Street, Charleston, SC 29401   843-577-0175

VIRGINIA

    1025 King Street, Alexandria, VA 22314   703-549-3806

CANADA

    3022 Dufferin Street, Toronto, ON M6B 3T5   416-781-9131

¡También somos su fuente para libros,
videos y música en español!

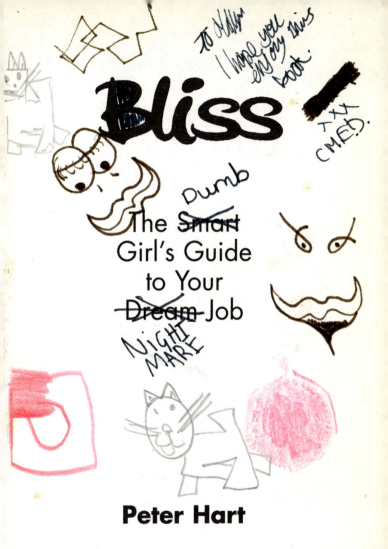

Bliss

The ~~Smart~~ Dumb Girl's Guide to Your ~~Dream~~ Job Nightmare

Peter Hart

Piccadilly Press • London

For Mum, Dad and Carolyn,
who never stopped believing that I'd get my dream job.

First published in Great Britain in 2000
by Piccadilly Press Ltd.,
5 Castle Road, London NW1 8PR

Photoypeset from the author's disk
in 10.5 Futura Book

A catalogue record for this book
is available from the British Libary

ISBN: 1 85340 642 2 (paperback)

1 3 5 7 9 10 8 6 4 2

Printed and bound in Great Britain
by Bookmarque Ltd

Design by Louise Millar

Peter Hart is the Features Editor of Bliss magazine.
He lives in New Cross, south-east London.
This is his first book.

CONTENTS